Be a Plant Scientist

Contents

Written by Michele Paul

What Do Plant Scientists Do?

Would you like to be a plant scientist? Plant scientists need to know lots of things about plants. One of the most important things they need to know is what things help plants grow.

Plant scientists find out what makes plants grow.

One way a plant scientist can find out what sorts of different things help plants grow is to carry out some experiments.

Plant scientists help farmers grow better crops.

Plants and Light Experiment

AIM: What do you want to find out?

Most of the plants you see growing around you seem to grow in the light, but what would happen if they only had a little bit of light?

Sunflowers turn towards the light.

MATERIALS: What will you need?

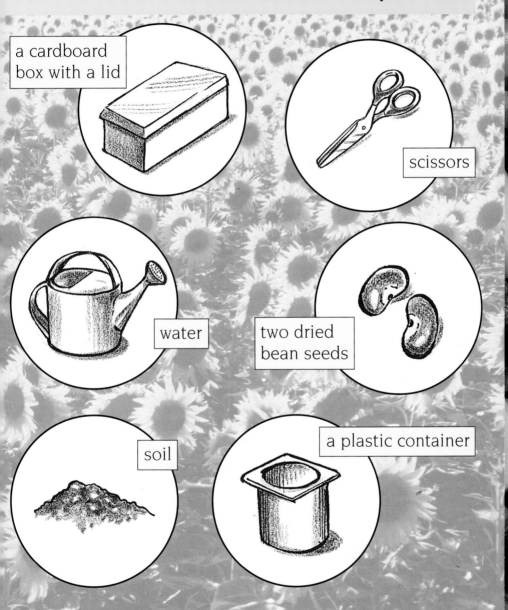

a cardboard box with a lid

scissors

water

two dried bean seeds

soil

a plastic container

METHOD: What will you do?

First cut a circle about the size of a can in one end of the box.

Fill the small container with soil and plant the bean seeds in the soil.

Put the container with the seeds into the end of the box without the hole.

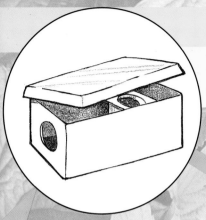

Put the lid back
onto the box.

Put the box in
a sunny position.

Water the seeds every
couple of days for a week.

CONCLUSION:
Think about your results.

What happened to the bean seeds?
What happened to the bean plants?
Why do you think this happened?

Plants and Water Experiment

AIM: What do you want to find out?

Most plants need water, but how do they get the water to their flowers?

MATERIALS: What will you need?

some water

dye, four different shades

four plastic cups

four white flowers, carnations are good

scissors

METHOD: What will you do?

First half fill the four
plastic cups with water.

Put three drops
of dye in each cup.
Use a different
shade for each cup.

Use the scissors to
trim the flower stems to
about 5 inches (13 cm) long.

Put one flower in each of the containers of water and dye.

Leave the flowers overnight.

CONCLUSION:
Think about your results.

What has happened?
Why has it happened?

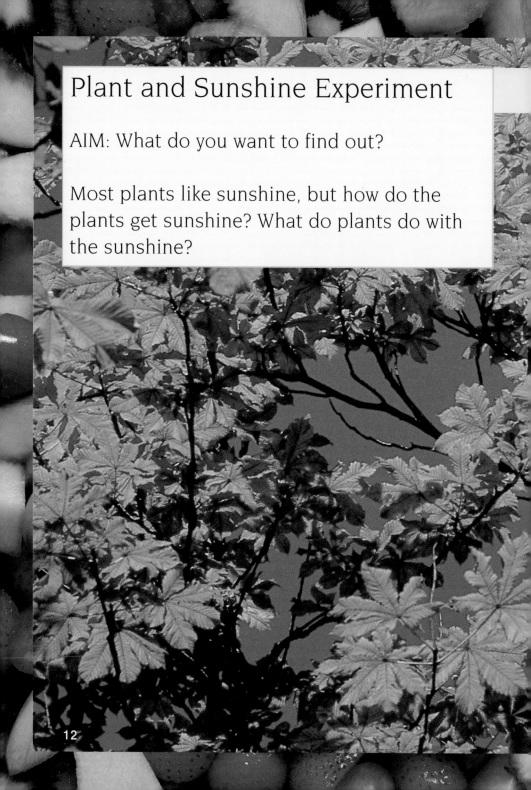

Plant and Sunshine Experiment

AIM: What do you want to find out?

Most plants like sunshine, but how do the plants get sunshine? What do plants do with the sunshine?

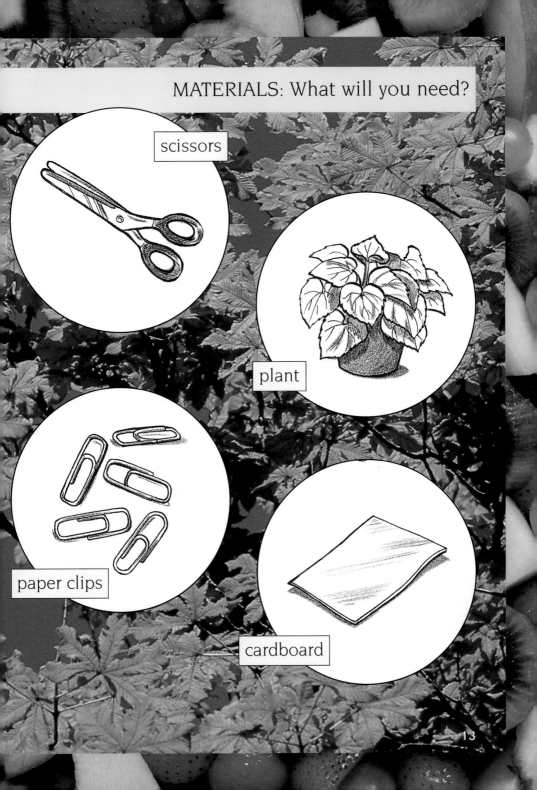

MATERIALS: What will you need?

scissors

plant

paper clips

cardboard

METHOD: What will you do?

Use the cardboard to cut some shapes that are smaller than the leaves of the plant.

Use the paper clips to clip the shapes over part of the plant's leaves. Do not cover all of the leaf.

Put the plant in a sunny spot. Water it every day.

Leave the cardboard shapes on the plant for a week, then take them off.

CONCLUSION:
Think about your results.

What has happened?
Why do you think this has happened?
What did you find out from your experiments?
Would you like to know more
about plants and become a real plant scientist?

Index